This
Book
Belongs To

_____

_____

1

CONTENTS PAGE

QUESTIONS NUMBER	ANSWERS page

GROUP-1

GROUP-2

GROUP-3

2

GROUP-4

Q. P : (106-112) -------------- A. (159)

Q. P : (113-120) -------------- A. (160)

Q. P : (120-127) -------------- A. (161)

GROUP-5

Q. P : (128-134) -------------- A. (162)

Q. P : (134-140) -------------- A. (163)

Q. P : (141-147) -------------- A. (164)

Fun Movie Trivia Questions

01. What was the name of the first film in the 'Harry Potter' series?

02. Which film's makeup and hairstyling won an Oscar despite the makeup budget being only $250?

03. In which movie did Keanu Reeves learn Judo, Brazilian Jiu-Jitsu, marksmanship and driving, and performed about 95% of the fight scenes himself?

04. In which movie was the iconic DeLorean time machine originally a refrigerator?

05. When adjusted for inflation, which is the highest-grossing movie of all time?

06. Which movie depicted the battle scenes of D-Day so realistically that it caused Post-Traumatic Stress Disorder in combat Veterans when they watched it?

07. Which movie has a Starbucks cup in every single scene in the movie?

08. Which is the First US film to Feature a toilet flushing?

09. After which movie did the sale of pet rats increase rapidly?

10. In which movie, was the sound of a Russian train's toilet flushing used as the sound of automatic doors opening?

11. In which movie did Leonardo DiCaprio have to devour a raw slab of bison's liver, despite being a vegetarian?

12. How many 'Star Wars' movies are there?

13. Which movie has a scene of two seconds of footage that took months to create?

14. Which movie's director was arrested for murder and had to prove himself innocent by calling in the actors that were "murdered"?

15. Which movie is the most death-packed film ever made with an average of five people dying every minute?

16. Steven Callahan, a real shipwreck survivor, helped film which movie as a technical advisor?

17. The roar made by a famous sci-fi creature was created by rubbing leather gloves on the strings of a musical instrument. Which sci-fi movie was this iconic roar from?

18. Which movies have over 24 minutes of just staring in them?

19. For which movie did Tim Burton train 40 squirrels to crack nuts for, rather than use CGI?

20. The directors of which movie wrote a new language, that the minions speak throughout the movie?

21. What are the dying words of Charles Foster Kane in Citizen Kane?

22. Who played Mrs. Robinson in The Graduate?

23. What was the first feature-length animated movie ever released?

24. In The Matrix, does Neo take the blue pill or the red pill?

25. For what movie did Tom Hanks score his first Academy Award nomination?

26. What 1927 musical was the first "talkie"?

27. What's the name of the skyscraper in Die Hard?

28. What flavor of Pop Tarts does Buddy the Elf use in his spaghetti in Elf?

29. What shocking Wes Craven horror movie carried the marketing tagline, "To avoid fainting, keep repeating, 'It's only a movie...'"?

30. What pop vocal group performs at the wedding in Bridesmaids?

31. What real-life on-again off-again Hollywood power couple starred in the film Who's Afraid of Virginia Woolf?

32. What American writer/director starred in several iconic European produced "Spaghetti Westerns"?

33. Who played Juror Number 8 in 12 Angry Men?

34. The head of what kind of animal is front-and-center in an infamous scene from The Godfather?

35. What TV show was Jack Nicholson referencing when he ad-libbed "Here's Johnny!" in The Shining?

36. What critically panned 1984 country musical comedy starring Dolly Parton and Sylvester Stallone eventually became a cult classic?

37. Who played park owner John Hammond in Jurassic Park?

38. In what 1976 thriller does Robert De Niro famously say "You talkin' to me?"

39. What's the name of the anthemic dance near the beginning of The Rocky Horror Picture Show?

40. For what movie did Steven Spielberg win his first Oscar for Best Director?

41. What is the name of the courtesan played by Nicole Kidman in Moulin Rouge!

42. In what 1950 drama does Bette Davis say, "Fasten your seatbelts; it's going to be a bumpy night"?

43. The theme from The Third Man (also called "The Harry Lime Theme" was performed on what instrument)?

44. Marlon Brando "could have been a contender" in what iconic 1954 crime drama?

45. What famous L.A. landmark is heavily featured in Rebel Without a Cause?

46. Who played Martin Luther King Jr. in the 2014 biopic Selma?

47. Who directed Boris Karloff in the classics Frankenstein and Bride of Frankenstein?

48. What infamous 1980 box-office bomb ruined the career of The Deer Hunter director Michael Cimino?

49. What words are written on the knuckles of "Reverend" Harry Powell (Robert Mitchum) in The Night of the Hunter?

50. What Hollywood movie star plays himself in Zombieland?

51. In Risky Business, what song did Tom Cruise famously lip-sync to in his underwear?

52. Who is the only actor to receive an Oscar nomination for acting in a Lord of the Rings movie?

53. Who took over the role of Bruce Wayne's love interest Rachel Dawes in The Dark Knight, following Katie Holmes's exit after Batman Begins?

54. What song plays over the opening credits of Guardians of the Galaxy?

55. For which 1964 musical blockbuster did Julie Andrews win the Academy Award for Best Actress?

56. What is the highest-grossing R-rated movie of all time?

57. What 1994 crime film revitalized John Travolta's career?

58. Who voiced the sultry Jessica Rabbit in Who's Afraid of Roger Rabbit?

59. Which movie was incorrectly announced as the winner of Best Picture at the 2017 Academy Awards, during the greatest Oscars flub of all time?

60. Which 1948 Alfred Hitchcock movie starred James Stewart and was shot to look like one continuous take?

61. "Well, nobody's perfect" is the final line (and punchline) from what classic 1959 comedy starring Marilyn Monroe?

62. The stage play Everybody Comes to Rick's was adapted for the screen to become what 1942 Best Picture winner?

63. In what 1979 James Bond movie does the famous spy go to outer space?

64. Who wrote the famous, scary theme music from Halloween?

65. What animated classic was the first film of the late-twentieth-century "Disney Renaissance?"

66. In Apocalypse Now, Robert Duvall says, "I love the smell of ____ in the morning."

67. What is the name of Quint's shark-hunting boat in Jaws?

68. What's the name of Charlie Chaplin's most famous, recurring character?

69. Aaron Sorkin won an Oscar for writing what 2010 drama about the creation of Facebook?

70. Who played iconic femme fatale Phyllis Dietrichson in classic 1946 film noir Double Indemnity?

71. What is the model of revolver made famous by Clint Eastwood's "Dirty" Harry Callahan?

72. Which 1927 war drama was the first movie to ever win Best Picture?

73. Who is the first actor to play Jack Ryan on screen?

74. What was Audrey Hepburn's birth name?

75. Joaquin Phoenix received his first Oscar nomination for playing Roman emperor Commodus in what 2000 Oscar-winning epic?

76. Who played the "Unsinkable" Molly Brown in Titanic?

77. In the action thriller Speed, why is Annie (Sandra Bullock)'s driver's license suspended?

78. Jennifer Lawrence won a Best Actress Academy Award for what 2012 romantic comedy/drama?

79. The Battle of Thermopylae served as the basis of what highly stylized 2006 smash hit swords-and-sandals action flick?

80. Which famous film composer wrote the music for Tim Burton's 1989 Batman?

81. Which Alfred Hitchcock thriller is notorious for its shocking "shower scene"?

82. What is the highest-grossing foreign-language film at the U.S. box office?

83. Who wrote the screenplay for Rocky?

84. What national monument does Cary Grant climb in the heart-pounding final moments of North by Northwest?

85. What was Quentin Tarantino's first feature as writer/director?

86. Which Oscar-winning blonde bombshell played James Stewart's love interest Lisa Carol Fremont in Rear Window?

87. Who is the only person ever to receive an Oscar nomination for acting in a Star Wars movie?

88. What actress' name, who voices Princess Elsa in the Frozen films, did John Travolta botch at the 2014 Oscars?

89. What is the real name of Uma Thurman's "The Bride" character from Kill Bill?

90. What prominent American director won an Oscar for helming Forrest Gump?

91. Three of Jim Carrey's blockbusters The Mask, Dumb and Dumber and Ace Ventura: Pet Detective—were all released in what year?

92. How many suns does Luke's home planet of Tatooine have in Star Wars?

93. What movie holds the record for most Oscar wins without winning Best Picture (eight wins total)?

94. In what 1969 James Bond thriller does the famous spy fall in love and get married?

95. What 1970 movie marked the feature debut of Arnold Schwarzenegger?

96. What is the first movie ever to be rated PG-13?

97. What is the highest-grossing movie of all time when taking inflation into account?

98. What is the highest-grossing movie of all time when not taking inflation into account?

99. What's the Los Angeles hotel prominently featured in Pretty Woman?

100. What is the only 'X'-rated film to win Best Picture at the Oscars?

101. Who played detective Rick Deckard in Blade Runner?

102. This acclaimed, Oscar-winning filmmaker directed Happy Feet, Babe: Pig in the City and Mad Max: Fury Road.

103. Who is the first and only woman of color to win the Oscar for Best Actress?

104. What's the fictional brand of cigarettes in Quentin Tarantino's movies?

105. Who played the Wicked Witch of the West in The Wizard of Oz?

106. Which movie star is killed off in the opening scene of Scream?

107. What's the name of John Wayne's character in True Grit (played by Jeff Bridgesin the remake)?

108. What is the highest-grossing war movie of all time and Clint Eastwood's highest-grossing movie ever?

109. How many Oscars has Meryl Streep been nominated for?

110. Who played Bonnie Parker and Clyde Barrow in Bonnie & Clyde?

111. What Martin Scorsese movie holds the all-time record for F-bombs?

112. What is the name of the extended ballet sequence near the end of Singin' in the Rain?

113. What is the name of Riley's imaginary friend in Inside Out?

114. Who played the Green Goblin in 2002 box-office smash Spider-Man?

115. For what movie did George Clooney win his sole acting Oscar to date?

116. Near the end of Vertigo, when Judy transforms into Madeline, she is bathed in what color light?

117. Who played Regan MacNeil in The Exorcist?

118. Only three movies in history have won the "big five" at the Oscars (Best Picture, Best Director, Best Screenplay, Best Actor and Best Actress). Name them.

119. What is the name of the spaceship in Alien?

120. How many Oscars has Meryl Streep won?

1. Which singer starred 1n' "The Bodyguard"?

2. Which actress Keaton starred in "Father of the Bride II"?

3. "I Saw the Light" was a 2016 biopic of which country music legend?

4. Which Holly won an Oscar for a silent role in "The Piano"?

5. Which silent movie star was played by Robert Downey Jr in 1992?

6. Which Welsh actor starred with Jodie Foster in "The Silence of the Lambs"?

7. Which Bob starred in "Mona Lisa" before finding it "good to talk"?

8. Which Steven directed "Schindler's List"?

9. Which actor Sylvester has the nickname Sly?

10. Who is Donald Sutherland's actor son?

11. What is the first name of "Pulp Fiction" director Tarantino?

12. Which actor won an Oscar as director of "I'Janc'es with Wolves"?

13. Which Nick co-starred with Barbra Streisand in "The Prince of Tides"?

14. What is the first name of actress Sarandon?

15. Which Johnny starred as Edward Scissorhands?

16. Why is Bill Murray's character (Bob) in Tokyo in the movie Lost in Translation (2003)?

17. In the French New Wave's most successful film, Jeanne Moreau's character (Catherine) falls in love with two men, Jules and Jim. Who directed the 1962 movie?

18. In which language was Crouching Tiger Hidden Dragon filmed?

19. On what date is the Frank Capra classic Its' a Wonderful Life set?

20. Who took the part of Mr Pink in Tarantino's Reservoir Dogs, a role the director had reportedly earmarked for himself?

21. Which novelist adapted Pride and Prejudice for Joe Wright's movie version?

22. Which electronic band composed all the music for Tron: Legacy in 2010?

23. Who plays corrupt sheriff Hank Quinlan in Orson Welles's Touch of Evil (1958)?

24. What is the name of the vegetation assessor that becomes the object of the hero's affection in WALL-E?

25. Which pair of real-life brothers (including first names) play the titular roles in The Fabulous Baker Boys (1989)? And what is the name of the alluring singer for whom they both fall, played by Michelle Pfeiffer?

26. Who got tetchy when British critics ridiculed his English accent in Ridley Scott's 2010 Robin Hood?

27. A Bronx Tale (1993) was the directorial debut of which Hollywood star?

28. Who was playing the I Am Legend?

29. In 1999 Gwyneth Paltrow won an Academy Award in a role in Shakespeare in Love that demanded she spent much of the film pretending to be a man; who replicated this feat the following year, and in which film?

30. Who won an Oscar nomination for his portrayal of American activist Malcolm X?

31. God bless America was a 2012 movie made by which comic film-maker and actor? In which movie franchise did he make his name?

32. Who plays Shaun's mum and stepdad in Shaun of the Dead? And what was the TV show made by the director Edgar Wright and Simon Pegg?

33. Apart from his mockery of Hitler as Adenoid Hynkel hat part was played by Chaplin in his own The Great Dictator (1940) The character Napolini in the same film was a parody of which other political figures?

34. Who or what is the 'baby' mentioned in the title of the 1938 comedy Bringing Up Baby?

35. What 1990s cult movie spawned fan festivals involving vast consumption of White Russian Cocktails? What are the two main ingredients of a White Russian?

36. What is the subtitle of Stanley Kubrick's 1964 satire of the military, Dr. Strangelove?

37. the Jerk, The Man with Two Brains, Dead Men Don't Wear Plaid and All of Me are collaborations between which star and director?

38. Who plays the body-swap mother and daughter in Freaky Friday (2003)?

39. Kareem Abdul-Jabaar features as a co-pilot in the hit 1980 comedy Airplane! For what was he better known?

40. Which film concerns the declaration of war by Freedonia against neighbouring Sylvania?

41. What are the full titles of the three Austin Powers movies? Who played both Powers and his nemesis, Dr Evil? Who appeared as Dr Evil's son, Scott?

42. What four games do Bill and Ted play against Death (and win) in Bill and Ted's Bogus Journey? Which classic European film is the scene spoofing?

43. If Sharon Stone betrayed an amnesiac Arnold Swarzenneger in Paul Verhoeven's 1990 version, who betrayed in 2012 version under Len Wiseman's direction?

44. Escape fromNew York (1981) The Thing (1982) and Big Trouble in Little China (1986) are all escapist melodramas involving which director/star combination?

45. Which comic book hero provided a big break for Mexican director Guillermo del Toro in 2004? What was the subtitle of the follow-up, released in 2008?

46. How many days did it take David Niven to go Around the World?

47. In the 1957 film about Japanese prisoners of war, where was the Bridge?

48. Which Ben won 11 Oscars in 1959?

49. In which 1940 film did Mickey Mouse conduct the orchestra?

50. In which film did Vivien Leigh play Scarlet O'Hara?

51. Who starred in the Road films with Dorothy Lamour and Bing Crosby?

52. Which distinguished actor, later a Lord, played the lead in 'Henry V'?

53. Which film starred Celia Johnson, Trevor Howard and a train station?

54. Which Alfred directed the thrillers 'Rebecca' and 'Notorious'?

55. Who played eight different characters in 'Kind Hearts and Coronets'?

56. What was the series of comedies made in West London studios called?

57. Which young star of 'East of Eden' died in a car crash aged 24?

58. Which actress married Prince Rainier of Monaco?

59. Which French 'sex kitten' starred with Dirk Bogarde in 'Doctor at Sea'?

60. In the Charlton Heston film, how many commandments were there?

61. Who starred as Cleopatra and married co-star Richard Burton?

62. Who was The Graduate in the film of the same name?

63. Who won an Oscar as Professor Higgins in 'My Fair Lady'?

64. Which musical by Lionel Bart was based on a Dickens novel?

65. Which western actor won his only Oscar for 'True Grit'?

66. Which nanny did Julie Andrews win an Oscar for playing?

67. Which Gregory won an Oscar for 'To Kill a Mockingbird'?

68. How many Dalmatians starred in the 1961 Disney Film?

69. Which 1960 Hitchcock film has the most famous shower scene ever?

70. Which 1972 film, with Marlon Brando, was about the Mafia?

71. Who is Clark Kent better known as?

72. Which 1970s film about a giant ape was a remake of a 1933 movie?

73. Which disaster movie was about a fire in the world's tallest building?

74. Who starred with Paul Newmann in 'The Sting'?

75. Which planet features in the title of a 1979 Bond movie?

76. Don Siegel in 1956 and Philip Kaufman in 1976 directed two versions of which classic horror movie?

77. Who directed the low-budget horror classic The Evil Dead in 1981? What was the name of the main protagonist played by Bruce Campbell?

78. Who starred in the defining 1958 Hammer Horror version of Dracula as the urbane but terrifying Count, and who played his nemesis, Van Helsing?

79. What was the compendium chiller movie made in 1945 at Ealing with Alberto Cavalcanti, Charles Crichton, Basil Dearden and Robert Hamer each directing a segment?

80. Which 1974 Tobe Hooper slasher movie had to wait twenty-five years to get a rating from the British Board of Film Classification?

81. Deborah Kerr is a governess who looks after two monstrous children, Flora and Miles in a disturbing 1960 creepy classic; Jack Clayton directs- what's the movie?

82. What was Hideo Nakata's 1998 horror classic, remade by Gore Verbinski in 2002?

83. What was the voyeuristic 1960 chiller that greeted with such opprobrium that it hampered director Michael Powell's career?

84. What was Elsa Lanchester's most famous role, in a James Whale directed film of 1935?

85. Which later-to-be-very-famous New Zealand director made the 1992 gross-out horror-comedy Braindead?

86. What was Tomas Alfredson's 2008 film, a bleak contemporary account of a vampire's existence set in a small town in Swedeen?

87. What was the name of the possessed girl, played by Linda Blair in the Exorcist?

88. Which film features Joe Turkel as Lloyd, a polite but sinister barman, and Lisa and Louise Burns as the young Grady Twins?

89. Who was the first victim of the psychotic killer in Halloween?

90. What was Kathrin Bigelow's 1987 cult movie about a blood-drinking family travelling across America?

91. What is the name of the villain in the first Superman movie (1980) played by Gene Hackman?

92. Which British comic actor played Scotty, the engineer abroad the Enterprise in Star Trek (2009)? And which Aussie was the bad guy Nero?

93. Who made Ray Bradbury's classic novel Fahrenheit 451 into a movie in 1966?

94. In 2005 both Steven Spielberg and Peter Jackson revisited classic sci-fi stories for the major movies; what were the two films?

95. Serve the trust. Protect the innocent. Uphold the law. whose mantra?

96. Which classic sci-fi movie concern the invention of a beautiful robot by a scientist called Rotwang?

97. In which movie David Bowie appears as Jareth the Goblin King?

98. What is Mad Max's surname? And who leads the gang that kills his family

99. Who played the obsessive character at the centre of Close Encounters of the Third Kind (1997)?

100. Who made the 1989 underwater sci-fi chiller The Abyss?

101. What was the 1982 film starring Jeff Bridges as a computer software programmer battling to escape from being trapped inside his own programme?

102. The 2013 Star Trek film brings the number of films in the official franchise up to eight, twelve or sixteen?

103. What was the name of the Duncan Jone's 2009 feature debut, and which actor carried the film almost single-handedly

104. Who remade Solaris in 2002 and who took the lead role? Which Russian director made the original thirty years earlier?

105. Who was The Invisible Man in James Whale's 1993 film? And on whose story was the film based?

106. Who won his second Oscar in successive years for Forrest Gump?

107. Which circus musical starred Glenn Close as the hero's wife on Broadway?

108. Which Ben and Matt co-wrote Good Will Hunting?

109. Who met husband Richard Burton on the set of Cleopatra?

110. In which blockbuster did Anthony Perkins first appear as Norman Bates?

111. Which Nick won an Oscar for The Wrong Trousers?

112. The King in the King and I is ruler of where?

113. Who or what is Gromit?

45

114. Who played Jack in Titanic?

115. Nigel Hawthorne was Oscar nominated for The Madness of which King?

116. Aspects of what was a success by Andrew Lloyd Webber?

117. Who was the Pretty Woman in the 1990 film with Richard Gere?

118. Which British actor / director Richard was Dr. Hammond in Jurassic Park?

119. Which musical based on Romeo & Juliet was a 60s Oscar winner?

120. Where was the Fiddler in the Musical's title?

121. Which Anna played Nick Leeson's wife in the film Rogue Trader about the fall of Barings Bank?

122. Whose name appears with Dracula in the title of the 1992 movie?

123. Who won his second Oscar for the role of Raymond in Rain Man?

124. If Sky and Nathan were Guys, what were Sarah and Miss Adelaide?

125. Which Kim did Alec Baldwin marry?

126. In which 70s film did "Love means never having to say you're sorry"?

127. Which Julie won an Oscar for Darling in 1965 and was Oscar nominated in 1998 for afterglow?

128. Which George wrote Crazy For You?

129. Who went to No 1 with Night Fever after writing the music for Saturday Night Fever?

130. Which film, the first of a series with Sigourney Weaver, had the line "In Space no one can hear you scream" on the cinema poster?

131. Raindrops Keep Falling On My Head was an Oscar winner from which movie with Robert Redford & Paul Newman?

132. In which decade did Godspell open on Broadway?

133. By which first name is Andrew Blyth Barrymore known?

134. Which Kevin starred in the spectacularly money-losing Waterworld?

135. In which film did Jodie Foster play FBI agent Clarice Starling?

136. South Pacific was set during which war?

137. Which film director was involved in a long-running custody battle for his children with Mia Farrow?

138. In which country did The Sound of Music take lace?

139. Which veteran actress Katharine was the first actress to win four Oscars?

140. Which show about Danny and Sandy was made into a film with John Travolta and Olivia Newton-John?

141. Which controversial 80s / 90s singer / actress married Sean Penn in 1985?

142. Which wartime classic, named after a port of North Africa starred Humphrey Bogart and Ingrid Bergman?

143. In 1997 James Cameron won an Oscar for which blockbuster?

144. Which actor starred in A Fistful of Dollars, Dirty Harry, and The Good, The Bad and The Ugly?

145. Which 2005 film tells the story of a lion, a hippo, a zebra and a giraffe who escape from Central Park Zoo?

146. Which instrument links characters played by Holly Hunter (1993) and Adrian Brody (2002) in films nominated for the Best Picture Oscar?

147. Which seminal 1978 musical movie was set in Rydell High School?

148. Which 1993 movie depicts a disaster at a wildlife park on the fictional Isla Nublar?

149. Scarlett O'Hara is the protagonist of which 1939 film?

150. Little Fockers is the third film in a series starring Ben Stiller and Robert DeNiro. What is the name of the first film in the series?

151. Which two actors played Don Corleone in the first two Godfather films?

152. Which festive movie from 1990 revolves around a character called Kevin McAllister?

153. Who directed Jaws, Empire of the Sun and the Indiana Jones series?

154. Which was the first feature film released by Walt Disney Animation Studios in 1937?

155. Which 1940 Disney film featuring Mickey Mouse was a series of animated scenes set to classical music?

156. Which 1942 movie includes a famous scene in which the protagonist struggles to find their footing on an icy lake?

157. Pongo and Perdita are the main good characters in which 1961 Disney movie?

158. What does Arthur effortlessly remove in the title of a 1963 movie, thus proving himself the heir to Uther Pendragon's throne?

159. Sebastian, Scuttle and Flounder are all supporting characters in which 1989 film?

160. Scott Weinger, Linda Larkin and Robin Williams were part of the cast of which 1992 Disney movie?

161. In which 1998 movie does a warrior's daughter pretend to be a man to take her father's place in the army?

162. Which 2010 Disney film is a retelling of the Rapunzel story?

163. In which 2016 film does the heroine have to restore the heart of Te Fiti?

164. Who played Vietnam veteran John Rambo in a famous series of action films that began in 1982?

165. In which 1996 movie do the surviving people of Earth launch a counterattack against their alien invaders on July 4th?

166. Which movie franchise portrays the trials and tribulations of Sarah and John Connor?

167. In which film does the protagonist write the message "Now I have a machine gun Ho-Ho-Ho" on a dead man's jumper?

168. Which film series has included The Last Stand, Apocalypse and Days of Future Past?

169. Who or what was responsible for three skinned corpses found hanging deep in a Central American jungle in a classic 1987 Arnie movie?

170. How were Martin Lawrence and Will Smith described in the title of a 1996 Action Comedy movie?

171. Which actor became an action hero aged 56 when he had to get his daughter back from Albanian traffickers in a 2008 movie?

172. Which film series that began in 1996 recounts the very difficult exploits of IMF agent Ethen Hunt?

173. In which film does Ryan Reynolds play Wade Wilson, an antihero on the hunt for the man who gave him mutant abilities?

174. Which character described himself as "loyal servant to the true emperor Marcus Aurelius, husband to a murdered wife, father to a murdered son" and promised to have his vengeance "in this life or the next"?

175. Julia Roberts, Bernie Mac, Don Cheadle, Andy Garcia, Brad Pitt, Matt Damon and George Clooney were all in a film together in 2001. What was it?

176. Which baby was curiously born looking like an old man according to the plot of a 2008 movie?

177. In which blockbuster was the human race trying to colonize a moon called Pandora in order to mine a mineral called "unobtanium"?

178. Who directed Inglourious Basterds and the two Kill Bill films?

179. Who played the British Prime Minister in the 2003 Richard Curtis film Love Actually?

180. Which American actress played the lead roles in Freaky Friday and Mean Girls?

181. Who starred as chilling assassin Anton Chigurh in the Coen brothers' movie No Country for Old Men?

182. Which highly successful 2008 musical comedy was largely filmed on the Greek island of Skopelos?

183. Where in the American West do Ennis and Jack get jobs as herders in Ang Lee's 2005 film?

184. Julie Andrews' Best Actress win came for playing the eponymous character in which musical?

185. Roberto Benigni won the Best Actor gong for which foreign language movie in 1998?

186. Jodie Foster's second Academy Award for Best Actress came for playing Clarice Starling in which film?

187. Rami Malek's Academy Award win in 2018 was for his portrayal of which singer?

188. Which actress won an Oscar for playing the lead role in psychological ballet drama Black Swan?

189. Which actress has been nominated the most times in the best actress category, winning for Sophie's Choice and The Iron Lady?

190. Who won the Best Actor Oscar twice in a row in 1993 and 1994?

191. For which film did Emma Stone win the gong in 2016, opposite Ryan Gosling?

192. Which actor won the 1975 Best Actor Oscar for playing the lead in One Flew Over the Cuckoo's Nest?

193. What happened seven times in the twentieth century, first with Clark Gable and Claudette Colbert for It Happened One Night?

194. Which 1979 action movie had the tagline "In Space, nobody can hear you scream"?

195. Which 2010 movie was promoted with "You don't get to 500 million friends without making a few enemies"?

196. Which shark film had the tagline "Just when you thought it was safe to go back in the water"?

197. "For Harry and Lloyd, every day is a no brainer" was the tagline for which 90s comedy?

198. Which British film was billed as "A romantic comedy, with zombies"

199. Which classic thriller had the tagline "Check in. Unpack. Relax. Take a shower."

200. "He is afraid, he is alone, he is 3 million light years from home" was the promotion line from which famous movie?

201. Which cult 80s comedy had the tagline "One man's struggle to take it easy"?

202. If there is something peculiar in your local environs, "Who ya gonna call?"

203. Which Jim Carrey movie was promoted with the line "On the Air. Unaware."

204. Tom Hanks plays a Vietnam veteran, two-time All-American sportsman and successful seafood entrepreneur who exposes the Watergate scandal and inspires Elvis Presley's dance moves.

205. In a real-life story, Tom Hanks is a newspaper editor who has to decide whether to publish shocking revelations about the Vietnam War.

206. Tom Hanks plays Walt Disney, trying to persuade the author of Mary Poppins to let him turn her books into film.

207. Tom Hanks leads an expedition in occupied France to try and bring back a soldier whose three brothers have all been killed.

208. Tom Hanks falls in love with a beautiful mermaid.

209. Tom Hanks plays a boy who finds himself in a man's body.

210. Tom Hanks agrees to offer himself as a human sacrifice on the Pacific island of Waponi Woo.

211. Tom Hanks plays an alcoholic ex-baseball player who coaches a women's team called the Peaches.

212. Tom Hanks plays Professor Robert Langdon, who appears to be implicated in a murder at the Louvre.

213. Tom Hanks plays an astronaut whose spacecraft suffers an explosion, depriving it of most of its oxygen.

214. Which film from 1994 has the famous line "Zed's dead, baby. Zed's dead." by one of the leading characters, Bruce?

215. The lines by the character Brody of "You're going to need a bigger boat", was from which 1975 film?

216. Bill apparently said "I love the smell of napalm in the morning" but in which 1979 war movie did this line become famous?

217. Rhett said "Frankly my dear, I don't give a damn" in which 1939 classic?

218. In which 1997 film did Jack shout the words "I'm the king of the world!"?

219. Michael believed that you should "Keep your friends close, but your enemies closer" in which 1974 film?

220. In which 1989 film did John exclaim "Carpe diem. Seize the day, boys. Make your lives extraordinary"?

221. In what film, released in 2008 was the line "May the odds be ever in your favour" uttered by Effy?

222. Nathan shouted in court that "You can't handle the truth!" in which 1992 movie?

223. A very sad moment as Chuck screamed "WILSON!!!" is a famous line from which movie from 2000?

224. Which Tom Cruise film featured Take My Breath Away and Highway to the Dangerzone on its iconic soundtrack?

225. Edelweiss, I am Sixteen going on Seventeen and Climb Every Mountain featured in which sixties musical film?

226. Which Tarantino film contains a famous torture scene to the sound of Stuck in the Middle with you by Stealers Wheel?

227. I Will Always Love You was one of the bestselling number ones of the nineties thanks to which film?

228. A piece of music called Dueling Banjos plays in a famous scene from which 1972 thriller starring Burt Reynolds?

229. A cover version of Lady Marmalade by Pink, Missy Elliot, Maya, Lil Kim and Christina Aguilera was on the soundtrack to which 2001 film?

230. (I've Had) The Time of My Life was the standout song from which 1987 soundtrack?

231. Pharrell William's smash hit Happy was first released as part of the soundtrack to which children's film sequel?

232. 90s bands such as Pulp and Sleeper performed on the soundtrack for which modern classic British film that also features the songs Lust for Life and Born Slippy.

233. Judy Garland's Somewhere Over the Rainbow was written for which 1939 movie?

234. Which iconic character, the spirit of a serial killer, was first portrayed in A Nightmare on Elm Street by Robert Englund?

235. In which film do Gregory Peck and Lee Remick raise a child called Damien who turns out to be the antichrist?

236. Which low budget 1999 horror film about some documentary makers hiking in the woods grossed nearly $250 million dollars worldwide?

237. Who played the beleaguered Sidney Prescott in the Scream films?

238. Which Jamie Lee Curtis horror classic was released in late October 1978?

239. On what date are a group of teens trying to reopen an abandoned summer camp murdered by Jason Voorhees' mother in a famous 1980 slasher movie?

240. What reversed word does Danny chant over and over in the Shining? Backwards it sounds like a famous horse and forwards, as his mother eventually notices in the bathroom mirror, it spells a crime.

241. Complete the titles of this horror trilogy that began in the 90s: I knowz; I still know...; I'll always know...

242. What sort of animals begin attacking the residents of Bodega Bay, California in a 1963 Hitchcock classic?

243. In which seminal horror movie do two priests try to remove a demon who has possessed a girl called Regan?

244. What year did the Shawshank Redemption get released?

245. What was the first movie with sound?

246. Who were the main actors in the Shawshank Redemption?

247. In the Shawshank Redemption, Morgan Freeman's character was nicknamed what?

248. How many Starwars movies have been released?

249. How many Academy Awards has Forrest Gump won?

250. The main character in Toy Story was voiced by which actor?

251. What is the most popular sports film in movie history?

252. What is the highest-grossing film of all time?

253. "I hate snakes" is a line from which movie?

254. It's a Wonderful Life was released in what year?

255. What is the only animated film to receive a Special Achievement Academy Award?

256. What was the first full-feature Disney movie?

257. "Get Out" is what genre of movie?

258. What year was Forrest Gump released?

259. What year was Batman & Robin released?

260. What character did Goerge Clooney play in Oceans 11?

261. What is the highest-grossing Star Wars movie?

262. What war movie won the Academy Award for Best Picture in 2009?

263. What is the highest-grossing animated film in movie history?

264. Julie Andrews made her feature film debut in which animated Disney movie?

265. What Indiana Jones film led to the creation of the movie rating "PG-13?"

266. What music artist sang "Oh, Pretty Woman" from the feature film Pretty Woman?

267. What was the first James Bond movie?

268. What type of car did 007 (James Bond) drive in the first James Bond movie?

269. What is the name of Will Smith's character in Men in Black?

270. Patrick Swayze is best known for lifting a girl above his head in what film?

271. In the film "Ghost," the couple is seen creating what type of art together?

272. What is the first sports film to win an Academy Award for Best Picture?

273. About how much money has the Star Wars movies grossed in the box office?

274. How many Disney films are in existence?

275. What year was the latest Lion King rendition released?

276. Who directed the horror film "Scream?"

277. Who was the first character to die in the horror film Psycho?

278. How many Academy Award wins did the film Schindler's List win?

279. How many Academy Awards has Joaquin Phoenix won?

280. In the movie, Forrest Gump, the name of his shrimping company was what?

281. In the movie "Sixth Sense," the child says he can see what?

282. What is the movie where Eddie Murphy's character works in a speakeasy?

283. Which actor played Forrest Gump's mother?

284. Chris tucker played which character in the 1998 film, "Rush Hour?"

284. In Will Smith's detective comedy starring Martin Lawrence, they have a slogan for themselves. They say, "___ for life." What is the blank phrase?

286. Hoosiers is about a basketball team located in what state?

287. In the movie Ferris Bueller, it takes place where?

288. In Ferris Bueller, what type of king does Ferris pretend to be?

289. What type of car do Ferris and his friend take from their parents?

290. Which actor starred as Ferris in Ferris Bueller's Day Off?

291. In the film "Pretty in Pink," where does Molly Ringwald's character work?

292. "Mess with the bull, get the horns" is a phrase from what movie?

293. How many fingers do they hold up as a type of salute in the Hunger Games movies?

294. Who is the name of the person who writes and directs all of their own movies? To have each film written and directed by themselves.

295. Zac Efron became a breakout star in which movie?

296. What was the last Indiana Jones movie to be released?

297. In the movie "17 Again," Zac Efron quits what team to become a father?

298. Which Disney princess dresses up as a man to save her father?

299. What year was the Jungle Book released?

300. Trivia Question: The Harry Potter trilogy has how many movies?

301. What was the first film to be released in the "PG-13" rating?

302. In the film "Frozen," what actor is the voice of Olaf?

303. In the movie "Usual Suspects," who plays the main character?

304. What movie did Robin Williams dress as a woman to be closer to his children?

305. In the movie Happy Gilmore, who was the name of his golf pro trainer that only had one hand?

306. What year was the first Lion King released?

307. How many Oscars was Forrest Gump nominated for?

308. In Harry Potter and the Half-Blood Prince, Rufus Scrimgeour replaces what?

309. What is the most popular Disney character?

310. How many Ghostbusters were part of the team in the movie, "Ghostbusters?"

311. Who is the male actor to win the most amount of "Best Actor" awards?

312. Who has won the most Academy Awards?

313. The Boondock Saints is about what?

314. What cult classic is known to be the absolute worst movie in history?

315. What is the best-selling soundtrack of all time?

316. Who was the lead character in the movie, "Big?"

317. In the movie "Big," Tom Hanks and his boss dance on what in the toy store?

318. The machine in the movie "Big" where the young boy casts his wish is named what?

319. How many hours did it take for Jim Carrey to get into costume in The Grinch Stole Christmas?

320. In the movie "Dumb and Dumber," where do Lloyd and Harry go?

321. In "Dumb and Dumber" what type of store do Lloyd and Harry want to start?

322. What was the first animated feature to be nominated for "Best Picture?"

323. What is the most popular Disney film?

324. What popular Disney character makes an appearance as a stuffed animal in "Frozen?"

325. What is the name of the young girl and sister in Jurassic Park?

326. What is shaking in Jurassic Park as they hear T-Rex coming?

327. In the Breakfast Club, where was the film recorded?

328. In what movie did John Candy play a vicarious uncle?

329. In "Planes, Trains, and Automobiles" the two are trying to get home for what holiday?

330. In "Home Alone" what is the name of the two bandits?

331. "Home Alone" was played by which child-star actor?

332. What was the first horror movie to come out as a feature film?

333. What is the current highest grossing film between the years 2010 and 2021?

334. Raiders of the Lost Ark is the name of a movie in what series?

335. Detective David Mills is a character in what movie featuring Brad Pitt?

336. What movie featured a surfing FBI agent played by Keanu Reeves?

337. What was Patrick Shwayze's character's name in the hit movie "Point Break?"

338. In the movie "Oldschool" what does Vince Vaughn recommend to put in the house?

339. In what movie does Vince Vaughn play a playboy who lives in Los Angeles?

340. Who is Vince Vaughn's costar in "Wedding Crashers?"

341. What state does the fictional city of Gotham take place in?

342. What was the first movie George Clooney starred in?

343. Brad Pitt is known as being a fictional figment/friend in what movie?

344. What decade did the popular movie "The Sandlot" take place?

345. What famous baseball player appeared in the dreams of the young boy in "The Sandlot?"

346. What was Leonardo DiCaprio's breakout role in?

347. What movie starred Michael Jordan and animated Looney Toons characters?

348. In what movie did Adam Sandler play an uncle who told fantasy stories?

349. How many movies has Adam Sandler directed?

350. What does Billy Madison have to accomplish in this Adam Sandler movie?

351. What was the last movie that Chris Farley starred in?

352. What year was the first "Wayne's World" movie released?

353. What was Dana Carvey's character's name in the movie "Waynes World?"

354. What were the only two horror movies to compete for an Oscar?

355. In the movie "Wayne's World," what Illinois city does it take place?

356. In the Raider's of the Lost Ark, what does Indiana jones potentially eat that has poison on it?

357. What Robin William's movie stars Robin as a robot?

358. In what Robin Williams movie does he go to heaven and learn he must save his wife?

359. When was Disney's Beauty and the Beast first released?

360. "Ya filthy animal" is a phrase from what movie?

1. The Man of Steel is another name for which superhero?
A. Batman
B. Superman
C. Iron Man

2. What is the real name of Batman?
A. Bruce Wayne
B. Bruce Davis
C. Bruce Devon

3. Batman protects which city?
A. Gotham City
B. Chicago
C. Metropolis

4. How did Spiderman have his superpowers?
A. He was born with the powers
B. He was affected by a chemical explosion
C. He was bitten by a spider

5. Which superhero said that "Who knows what evil lurks in the hearts of men?"

A. The Thing

B. The Shadow

C. The Devastator

6. The "Scarlett Speedster" is the nickname of which superhero?

A. Speedball

B. The Flash

C. Stardust

7. Which of the following superheroes says that "Don't make me angry; you wouldn't like me when I'm angry"?

A. Flash

B. Batman

C. Hulk

8. Which superhero has super tools such as the magic lasso and bullet proof bracelets?

A. Catwoman
B. Wonder Woman
C. Super Girl

9. In addition to Hal Jordan and Alan Scott, The Green Lantern also uses which name as a secret identity?

A. Kyle Rayner
B. Barry Allen
C. Britt Reid

10. Which superhero has an indestructible shield?

A. The Red Tornado
B. Captain Flag
C. Captain America

11. Which character is usually romantically paired with Batman?

A. Hawkgirl
B. Catwoman
C. The Black Canary

12. Which superhero cannot transform back into the human form anymore?

A. The Incredible Hulk
B. Jacob
C. The Thing

13. Who was the first female superhero of the Justice Society of America?

A. Wonder Woman
B. Storm
C. Elecktra

14. What villain got his distinctive appearance from toxic chemicals at a plant?

A. Joker
B. Doomsday
C. Two-Face

15. Raymond Palmer is the alter ego of which superhero?

A. The Green Arrow
B. Hawkman
C. The Atom

16. Which superhero says: "With great power, there must also come great responsibility"?

A. Batman
B. The Hulk
C. Spiderman

17. Which superhero is blinded by radioactive components and nicknamed the "Man without fear"?

A. Green Lantern
B. Daredevil
C. Wolverine

18. The Beast – a genius superhero – is the medical doctor for ... X-men.

A. X-men
B. Ice Man
C. Shadowcat

19. Barbara Gordon, the father of Batgirl, is the ... of Gotham City.

A. The mayor
B. The governor
C. The police chief

20. The Green Lantern gains his power from which object?

A. A ring
B. A necklace
C. Glasses

21. Which of the following superhero can manipulate and resist the weather?

A. The Tornado
B. The Atom
C. Strom

22. Wonder Woman comes from which island?

A. The Paradise Island
B. The Emerald Island
C. The Eden Isle

23. Where does the Green Arrow
mainly operate?

A. Gotham City
B. Star City
C. New York City

24. During the World War II, Steve
Rogers was given a special serum
that made him become ... to help
the US win the war.

A. The Hulk
B. Captain America
C. Wolfman

25. Which member of the Fantastic Four
has the tagline as "It's
clobbering time"?

A. The Thing
B. The Green Lantern
C. Iron Man

26. Debuting in 1965, which superhero is also known as Goliath and Ronin?

A. Hawkeye
B. The Beast
C. Iron Man

27. Which newspaper does Spiderman Peter Parker – work for?

A. The Daily Bugle
B. The Daily Gothamite
C. The Daily Planet

28. Elektra made her debut in which Marvel comic?

A. Green Lantern
B. Captain America
C. Daredevil

29. What is the name of the archnemesis of the Fantastic Four?

A. Llan the Sorcerer
B. Count Nefaria
C. Dr. Doom

30. In an attempt to look more normal, Hellboy did what of the following thing?

A. Fly down his horns
B. Wears contacts
C. Hide the right devil hand

31. Which of the following superheroes is a member of the JLA or Justice League of America?

A. Aquaman
B. Apache Chief
C. Storm

32. What are the claws of Wolverine made of?

A. Cadmium
B. Adamantium
C. Titanium

33. On the cover of a comic book in 1942 who was punched by Spy Smasher?

A. Axis leaders
B. Captain America
C. Uncle Sam

34. Doom, the enemy of Fantastic Four, stole the Power Cosmic from which villain?

A. Count Abyss
B. Galactus
C. Living Monolith

35. Which Spiderman villain shows up two times, first as a secret crime boss and then as a vengeance-bent son?

A. Green Goblin
B. Mysterio
C. Venom

36. Wonder Woman was formed by an expert in which field?

A. Psychology
B. Dentistry
C. Criminal justice

37. How does The Fantastic Four get their superpowers?

A. Evil curse
B. Genetic manipulation
C. Cosmic rays

38. With the special memory fibre in his cape, Batman is able to ...

A. Communicate with Batmobile
B. Slowly fall
C. Disappear

39. In Wonder Woman 1984, what is the civil job of the main character, Diana Prince?

A. A teacher
B. A librarian
C. An archaeologist

40. Which leading man rejects the role of Han Solo?

A. Mel Gibson
B. Al Pacino
C. Dustin Hoffman

41. Which character has the damaged mask of Darth Vader in "The Force Awakens"?

A. Finn
B. Rey
C. Kylo Ren

42. What is the name of Chewbacca's father?

A. Itchy
B. Scratchy
C. Harry

43. Which group invented the Death Star, the most powerful weapon in the universe?

A. Rebel Alliance
B. Galactic Empire
C. Ewoks

44. What is the main job of R2-D2?

A. Fighter pilot
B. Mechanic
C. Nurse

45. Where did the term "soap opera" operate from?

A. The first show was about a soap seller
B. Soap manufacturers originally sponsored these shows
C. Soaps were originally used in film production

46. First broadcast in 1950, which is the longest-running radio soap opera in the world?

A. Waggoners Walk
B. Front Line Family
C. The Archers

47. Many scholars consider "Painted Dreams" to be the first soap opera in the world. When was this program premiered?

A. 1930
B. 1935
C. 1940

48. In which English city does the soap opera "Brookside" set in?

A. Manchester
B. Liverpool
C. Newcastle

49. Which of the following TV soaps stars Jason Donovan and Kylie Minogue?

A. Neighbours
B. Family Affairs
C. Brookside

50. In the soap Coronation Street, how many kids does Steve Mc Donald have?

A. 1
B. 2
C. 3

51. In the soap EastEnders, Sonia Fowler is able to play which musical instrument the best?

A. Piano
B. Trumpet
C. Drum

52. What did Nick do for a living in the soap "Heartbeat"?

A. Detective
B. Police officer
C. Firefighter

53. In the soap Hollyoaks, the pub is called "... in the Pond"

A. The Dog
B. The Fish
C. The Cat

54. Who is the mother of the twins Chatham and Riley in the soap EastEnders?

A. Sandra Carter
B. Mia Hutchinson
C. Karen Taylor

55. Which of the following TV soaps was first premiered on 9th December 1960?

A. Emmerdale Farm
B. Crossroads
C. Coronation Street

1. What animal was framed in the unfinished paint-by-number in Rizzo's room in Grease?

2. What was the name of the boat in Jaws?

3. What are the names of the stepsisters from Disney's Cinderella?

4. Who was the first African American to win the Academy Award for best actor?

5. What is a nickname for the Academy Awards?

6. Which James Bond movie was the first for Pierce Brosnan as 007?

7. What year did Sean Connery star in the James Bond movie Dr. No?

8. Which film written, directed, and produced by James Cameron went on to become the highest-grossing film of its time?

9. Who directed the movie Schindler's List?

10. How many Oscars did the film Schindler's List win?

11. For which films did Tom Hanks receive an Academy Award for Best Actor?

12. Which Disney movie was the first full-length, animated feature produced in the United States?

13. What popular Disney character makes an appearance as a stuffed animal in the film Frozen?

14. In the Disney film The Little Mermaid, what does Ariel call the fork in her collection of human objects?

15. Which Disney princess dresses up as a man to save her father?

16. Who was the only non-Jedi in the original Star Wars trilogy to use a ightsaber?

17. Approximately how many languages can C-3PO speak in Star Wars?

18. In Rogue One, what is the Empire removing from the holy city on Jedha?

19. What was the name of the character Jack Nicholson played in the film One Flew Over the Cuckoo's Nest?

20. Who was the first actress to ever win an Academy Award?

21. Which actress has the longest TV career spanning over 80 years?

22. Which actress has won the most Academy Awards in history?

23. What is the current highest-grossing film of all time?

24. Who played the voice of Dory in the film Finding Dory?

25. What is the highest-grossing animated film in history?

26. Which actress won an Oscar for her first film role in Mary Poppins?

27. Which plant was actress Uma Turman named after in the film Batman & Robin?

28. Which 1994 film won an Oscar for Best Costume Design?

29. What is Indiana Jones' weapon of choice?

30. Which Indiana Jones film sparked the controversy that led to the creation of the PG-13 rating?

31. How old was Indiana Jones when his mother died?

32. How many hours did it originally take to get Jim Carrey to look like the Grinch for the film How the Grinch Stole Christmas?

33. In what year was Jim Carrey's first film released?

34. Which movie is the first non-English language film to win an Oscar for Best Picture?

35. Who was the first solo female host of the Oscars?

36. Which actor starred in the 1961 movie The Hustler?

37. In which year were the Academy Awards first presented?

38. How many times was actor Leonard DiCaprio nominated for an Oscar before winning Best Actor in 2016?

39. How many times has the movie A Star is Born been remade?

40. Who starred in the original version of the film A Star is Born?

41. How many Academy Awards has actress Meryl Streep been nominated for, and how many has she won?

42. What is the name of Repunzal's chameleon in Disney's movie Tangled?

43. Which actor danced his way to fame in the original version of Footloose?

44. What is Stephen King's top-grossing movie?

45. How many Nicholas Sparks books have been adapted into films?

46. What year did Noah and Ally meet in the film The Notebook?

47. In the film Rocky, what are Rocky's pet turtles' names?

48. What kind of flower was enchanted and dying in the movie Beauty and the Beast?

49. In The Fellowship of the Ring, what is the name of the ferry the hobbits use to escape the black riders?

50. Where was the entire trilogy of Lord of the Rings filmed?

51. How old was the actress Kate Hudson in the film Almost Famous?

52. What is the symbolism of the crow crowing three times in the Godfather movies?

53. What is the first song you hear in Disney's The Lion King?

54. What was Burt's profession in Mary Poppins?

55. What is the very first animal seen in Disney's The Lion King?

56. In what year was the film Good Will Hunting released?

57. How many movies are in the Jurassic Park series?

58. Who played Keyser Soze in the film The Usual Suspects?

59. What were the children's names in Mary Poppins?

60. In the movie The Usual Suspects, what is the greatest trick the devil ever pulled?

61. What animal is the handle of Mary Poppins' umbrella?

62. Who starred as Private Ryan in the movie Saving Private Ryan?

63. During which war is Saving Private Ryan set?

64. How many Oscars was the film Saving Private Ryan nominated for?

65. Who played Celie in the movie The Color Purple?

66. In the film Titanic, where was Jack Dawson from?

67. What was the treasure hunter team searching for in the ruins of the Titanic in the film

68. In The Matrix, on what level do Neo and Trinity stop the elevator after the lobby shootout?

69. Who directed the horror film Psycho?

70. Who was the first character to die in the horror film Psycho 3?

71. In which American city does the film Psycho begin?

72. What is the name of Edward Norton's character in Fight Club?

73. What is the name of the possessed hotel in the horror film The Shining?

74. What does "red rum" stand for in The Shining?

75. Who is the director of When Harry Met Sally?

76. Where were Harry and Sally driving when they first met in When Harry Met Sally?

77. In which year was Ferris Beuller's Day Off released?

78. In which American city does Ferris Beuller's Day Off take place?

79. How many children did Miss Celie have in The Color Purple?

78. What was Celie's husband's name in The Color Purple?

81. In the movie The Breakfast Club, why is Bender in detention?

82. Who opens the door to the ballroom when Maria is dancing around in The Sound of Music?

83. What is the youngest child's name in the von Trapp family in the film The Sound of Music?

84. How many children are in the von Trapp family in The Sound of Music?

85. Whose liver did Hannibal Lector eat aside fava beans and a nice chianti in the film The Silence of the Lambs?

86. What is the psychiatrist's name at the prison where Hannibal Lector lives in The Silence of the Lambs?

87. What dress size was Catherine Martin in The Silence of the Lambs?

88. What is Scarlett O'Hara's first name in Gone With the Wind?

89. In the movie Gone With the Wind, which Oscar-winning actress played Mammy?

90. How did Scarlett and Rhett's daughter die in Gone With the Wind?

91. What was Scarlett and Rhett's daughter's name in the film Gone With the Wind?

92. What were Rhett's last words to Scarlett in the film Gone With the Wind?

93. What was the name of the plantation where Scarlett lived in the film Gone With the Wind?

94. In what year was the film Forrest Gump released?

95. How long did Forrest run in the film, Forrest Gump?

96. In what year did Jenny die in the film, Forrest Gump?

97. What is Forrest's hometown in the film Forrest Gump?

98. What is Bubba's name in Forrest Gump?

99. Who starred as Lieutenant Dan in Forrest Gump?

100. What was Jenny and Forrest's son's name in Forrest Gump?

101. At the beginning of Back to the Future (Part 1), how many minutes slow is Doc's clock?

102. In Back to the Future, what type of car is the time machine?

103. In what year was the film The Shawshank Redemption released?

104. What is the total number of women who speak in the film The Shawshank Redemption?

105. What are the last two words in the film The Shawshank Redemption?

106. What is Red's full name in the film The Shawshank Redemption?

107. What is the group's name that assaulted Andy in prison in the film The Shawshank Redemption?

108. Which actor stars as Deadpool in Marvel's Deadpool?

109. Which actor received an Oscar for his portrayal of the Joker?

110. The film, The Proposal, takes place in which part of Alaska?

111. In which movie would you find the quote: "Exercise gives you endorphins. Endorphins make you happy. Happy people just don't shoot their husbands.
They just don't."?

112. In which Mission Impossible film did Tom Cruise train himself to do 6.5-minute breath holds?

113. Which 2018 film features the actor John Krasinski starring alongside his real-life wife, Emily Blunt?

114. How much weight did actress Anne Hathaway have to drop to portray Fantine in the 2012 film Les Misérables?

115. In which movie from the Underworld series do we see Selene and Michael's hybrid daughter?

116. In the animated movie Rio, which rapper voices Pedro, the cardinal?

117. Where is "Brokeback Mountain" in the film Brokeback Mountain?

118. Which actor stars as Ennis Del Mar in the film Brokeback Mountain?

119. In the movie Superbad, what kind of lunchbox does young Seth keep his taboo drawings in?

120. Attempting to explain himself to Donkey, Shrek compares himself to what?

121. In the animated film Cars, what is the name of Lightning McQueen's friend who is a tow truck?

122. In Kung Fu Panda, Poe's adopted father, Mr. Ping, is a what?

123. Who directed the film Get Out?

124. From which movie comes the quote, "I felt it. Perfect. I was perfect."?

125. Which social network is the film The Social Network based on?

126. Who played the voice of the genie in Disney's Aladdin?

127. In Finding Nemo, who says, "Fish are friends, not food."?

128. How many tribes originally settled in Wakanda, the land from the film Black Panther?

129. What is T'Challa's suit able to store in the film Black Panther?

130. How many fingers do they hold up as a salute in the Hunger Games Trilogy?

131. In the Hunger Games Trilogy, what is the name of the day the tributes are chosen?

132. In the film The Hunger Games, what berry are Katniss and Peeta going to eat when they discover they both cannot win?

133. What are the movies' titles within the superhero trilogy created by director M. Night Shyamalan?

134. What is the number on the roof of the bus in the film Speed?

135. What is the first sports film to win an Academy Award for Best Picture

136. What was the name of the young girl in the film Jurassic Park?

137. What war movie won the Academy Award for Best Picture in 2009?

138. What is the name of the kingdom where the 2013 animated movie Frozen is set?

139. Which English actor won the 2014 Academy Award for Best Actor in the film The Theory of Everything?

140. What was the name of Bella and Edward's daughter in the film Twilight: Breaking Dawn (Part 1)?

141. What is the last name of Edward and his family in the Twilight series?

142. In which film did actor Brad Pitt star as David Mills?

143. What are the four houses at Hogwarts School of Witchcraft and Wizardry in the Harry Potter series?

144. In The Lord of the Rings, what is the name of the elf that takes part in the fellowship of the ring?

145. The film Pulp Fiction was released in which year?

146. Who wrote the book that The Godfather is based on?

147. How long does Red spend in prison before being paroled in The Shawshank Redemption?

148. John Singleton is the youngest person to be nominated for Best Director at the Oscars. For which film was he nominated?

149. What is the name of the opening number from 2016 musical La La Land

150. What was the highest grossing film of 2019?

1. What is the name of the actor who plays the new 007 in the upcoming Bond film No Time To Die?

2. How many Steven Spielberg films has Tom Hanks starred in?

3. In 2013, Lupita Nyong'o became the first Kenyan and Mexican actress to win an Academy Award – which film did she win it for?

4. The Dig – the 2021 Netflix film starring Carey Mulligan and Ralph Fiennes – is about the real-life excavation of which Suffolk-based estate?

5. Inigo Montoya is a character from which 1987 Rob Reiner film?

6. What year was the first Toy Story film released in cinemas?

7. Who directed Titanic, Avatar and The Terminator?

8. Which three films make up what is known as the Three Flavours Cornetto Trilogy?

9. Who directed Parasite – the first foreign-language film to win the Academy Award for Best Picture?

10. Which Oscar-winning actress is the voice of Helen Parr (Elastigirl) in The Incredibles?

11. Name the 2015 film spinoff to the Rocky series starring Michael B. Jordan.

12. Meryl Streep won a Best Actress BAFTA for which 2011 political drama?

13. BD Wong voices Captain Li Shang in the animated musical Mulan, but which 70's teen heartthrob provided the character's singing voice?

14. Which actor broke two toes whilst filming The Lord of the Rings: The Two Towers?

15. Name the three movies in which Meg Ryan and Tom Hanks have starred together.

16. What is the highest-grossing box office film of all time?

17. Russell Crowe turned down the role of which character in Peter Jackson's Lord of the Rings trilogy?

18. How many films have Kate Winslet and Leonardo DiCaprio starred in together?

19. Name the film which boasts the famous line: "You can't handle the truth!"

20. What is the first word spoken in Star Wars: The Empire Strikes Back?

21. Who has won the most Oscars for acting in the history of the Academy Awards?

22. Which 1995 submarine drama featured uncredited additional dialogue courtesy of Quentin Tarantino?

23. Who played the lead role in the 2001 film Lara Croft: Tomb Raider?

24. Who was the director of 1996 action thriller The Rock?

25. What is the name of Tom Hanks' directorial debut which charts the rise and fall of a one-hit-wonder band in the 1960s?

26. In 1994 romcom Four Weddings and a Funeral, whose funeral does the group attend?

27. Who plays the titular role in 2018 superhero film Black Panther?

28. Which US comedian wrote and directed Get Out and Us?

29. What is the name of Wes Anderson's upcoming comedy drama starring Benicio del Toro, Tilda Swinton and Timothée Chalamet?

30. What is the name of the second James Bond film?

31. What is the name of the spell used by Ron and Hermoine in Harry Potter and the Philosopher's Stone to make their feathers fly?

32. What happens to Chihiro's parents in the 2001 Japanese film Spirited Away?

33. In '90s romcom Clueless, who plays Josh Lucas – Cher Horowitz's ex-step-brother?

34. How many Academy Awards has Leonardo DiCaprio won?

35. Which actor got his big break playing a lonely schoolboy in About A Boy?

36. For which film did Sandra Bullock win her Oscar?

37. Cool Runnings is the story of which country entering a bobsleigh team into the Winter Olympics?

38. 'Frankly my dear, I don't give a damn' is an iconic line from which classic film?

39. Emma Thompson made the nation cry in Love Actually – she thought her husband had bought her a necklace, but instead she received an album by which artist?

40. Who replaced Richard Harris as Dumbledore in the Harry Potter films?

41. What does Tom Hanks compare life to in Forest Gump?

42. Which movie features an iconic dance scene between Uma Thurman and John Travolta?

43. In which Austin Powers film does Beyoncé make her movie debut?

44. Who does Will Ferrell play in Anchorman?

45. In Indiana Jones and the Temple of Doom, which Star Wars character gets a namecheck?

46. What is the name of Humphrey Bogart's character in Casablanca?

47. Who is Alan Smithee?

48. What was Orlando Bloom's first film role?

49. Which Shakespearean actor directed the first Thor movie?

50. How many films have Al Pacino and Robert De Niro starred in together?

51. The Magnificent Seven is a remake of which iconic Japanese film?

52. What are the names of the twins played by Lindsay Lohan in the 1998 film The Parent Trap?

53. Which Alfred Hitchcock film starred Grace Kelly as Lisa Carol Fremont?

54. Who became the first woman to win a Best Director Oscar in 2010?

55. Who starred as Neil Armstrong in Damien Chazelle's biopic First Man?

56. Which was originally supposed to be revealed as the hunter who shot Bambi's mother in Who Framed Roger Rabbit?

57. Which was almost cut from The Little Mermaid?

58. Who is the youngest Disney villain at age 23?

59. How long it would be if Brave's Merida straightened her curly hair?

60. Who is the only Disney princess with a tattoo?

61. How would Ariel and Hercules are related?

62. Which one is estimated to be the most expensive film ever made, with Tangled(!) coming in at number two?

63. Who was supposed to be the villain in Frozen, but the producers loved "Let It Go" so much as an empowering anthem that they changed her storyline?

64. Who is the only title character that never speaks in a film?

65. During the end fight in which movie, Gaston's original line was "time to die!"?

66. Who auditioned three times for the role of Tiana in Princess and the Frog as Beyoncé reportedly refused to audition and expected to just be offered the part?

67. The appearance of which character was modeled after Tom Cruise, but he was originally supposed to be modeled after Michael J. Fox?

68. Who voices Lilo in Lilo and Stitch, also the actress who played Samara in The Ring. AKA, the scariest little girl of all time?

69. There are a total of 6,469,952 spots in___

70. Who has the largest eyes out of all the Disney princesses?

71. Sebastian from which movie almost had a British accent?

72. A deleted scene from which movie revealed that in earlier concepts of the film, Ursula was meant to be Triton's sister and Ariel's aunt?

73. Which was the first animated film in history to be nominated for a Best Picture at the Academy Awards?

74. Fans have been debating this since the movie came out: If Olaf had melted for Anna, would that act of true love have saved her? Which movie is all about?

75. Joss Whedon, one of the writers on which film, created the character of Rex the nervous dinosaur.

76. Who is the princess with the least amount of lines and screen time in a Disney film?

77. Before Meeko, who was supposed to have a talking turkey named Redfeather as a sidekick?

78. The little piece of hair that constantly falls in whose face is an intentional character detail added so it showed that she wasn't perfect?

79. Who from Finding Nemo was named after the animatronic shark used while filming Jaws?

80. What are the only animated Disney movies where the parents are both alive and present during the film?

81. What is the original name of Mickey Mouse?

82. Until Merida in Brave, who was the only Disney princess to have siblings?

83. Walt Disney said his favorite piece of animation is

84. Who is the only Disney princess to have a child. Her name is Melody?

85. Whenever he lies, you'll notice the feather on his turban falls in his face. Who is he?

86. The muses in which movie were intended to be voiced by The Spice Girls?

87. Who was the inspiration for Ariel's features?

88. Who voiced the character of Thomas in Pocahontas?

89. Who is the only Disney princess with hazel eyes?

90. Even though we know him as Prince Charming, we never actually find out the real name of the Prince character in the film

91. The queen in which movie is also never actually given a name?

92. Who provided the voice (both speaking and singing) for the Beast in the Chinese version of Beauty and the Beast?

93. Who is the first Disney character to ever fart onscreen, but we're sure plenty of other Disney characters fart in private?

94. Which famous band almost had roles in a Disney movie. They were meant to be the voices of the vultures in The Jungle Book?

95. In the Disney film Snow White, who is disguised as an old woman?

96. In which Disney film is Jafar a villain?

97. In which movie "Can You Feel the Love Tonight?" was originally supposed to be performed by Timon and Pumba?

98. What kind of food does the evil witch offer Snow White?

99. Who is Marlin?

100. What is the real name of Boo from Monsters, Inc.'s?

101. Which three films did James Dean star in?

102. Who wrote the score for 1994 Disney film The Lion King?

103. When was the National Television Awards' Most Popular Entertainment TV Presenter category won by someone other than Ant and Dec?

104. What is the name of the Christmas hit written by Will Brewis' (Hugh Grant) father in comedy About a Boy?

105. Which American comedy series has won a record 37 Emmy Awards?

106. What is the title of the first ever Game of Throne episode?

107. What is the name of the pub featured in UK soap Emmerdale

108. What are the names of the two winners of Love Island series 1

109. What was the most watched Netflix original TV series of 2019?

110. The Wire is set in which US city?

111. What is the population of David Lynch's idiosyncratic town Twin Peaks?

112. Which key Breaking Bad character was famously meant to die in series one?

113. What are the dying words of Charles Foster Kane in Citizen Kane?

114. In The Matrix, does Neo take the blue pill or the red pill?

115. For what movie did Steven Spielberg win his first Oscar for Best Director?

116. Which is the only foreign film to wine Best Picture at the Oscars?

117. Which veteran actors starred in the lead roles of True Detective, season one.

118. What is the first name of Zoolander's title character?

119. Mary Poppins is nanny to which family?

120. Which actor chipped a tooth making Fight Club?

01. 'Harry Potter And The Philosopher's Stone'.

02. 'Dallas Buyers Club'.

03. 'John Wick: Chapter 2'.

04. 'Back To The Future'.

05. 'Gone With The Wind'.

06. 'Saving Private Ryan'.

07. 'Fight Club'.

08. 'Psycho'.

09. 'Ratatouille'.

10. 'Star Trek'.

11. 'The Revenant'.

12. 12.

13. 'Transformers: Revenge Of The Fallen'.

14. 'Cannibal Holocaust'.

15. '300'.

16. 'Life Of Pi'.

17. 'Godzilla' (1954).

18. 'Twilight' series.

19. 'Charlie And The Chocolate Factory'.

20. 'Despicable Me'.

21. "Rosebud"

22. Anne Bancroft

23. Snow White and the Seven Dwarfs

24. Red

25. Big

26. The Jazz Singer

27. Nakatomi Plaza

28. Chocolate

29. The Last House on the Left

30. Wilson Phillips

31. Elizabeth Taylor and Richard Burton

32. Clint Eastwood

33. Henry Fonda

34. A horse

35. The Tonight Show Starring Johnny Carson

36. Rhinestone

37. Richard Attenborough

38. Taxi Driver

39. "The Time Warp"

40. Schindler's List

41. Satine

42. All About Eve

43. Zither

44. On the Waterfront

45. Griffith Observatory

46. David Oyelowo

47. James Whale

48. Heaven's Gate

49. "Love" and "hate."

50. Bill Murray

51. "Old Time Rock and Roll" by Bob Seger

52. Ian McKellen

53. Maggie Gyllenhaal

54. "Come and Get Your Love" by Redbone

55. Mary Poppins

56. Joker

57. Pulp Fiction

58. Kathleen Turner

59. La La Land

60. Rope

61. Some Like it Hot

62. Casablanca

63. Moonraker

64. John Carpenter

65. The Little Mermaid

66. Napalm

67. The Orca

68. "The Tramp"

69. The Social Network

70. Barbara Stanwyck

71. Smith & Wesson Model 29 .44 Magnum

72. Wings

73. Alec Baldwin

74. Audrey Kathleen Ruston

75. Gladiator

76. Kathy Bates

77. She was speeding

78. Silver Linings Playbook

79. 300

80. Danny Elfman

81. Psycho

82. The Passion of the Christ

83. Sylvester Stallone

84. Mount Rushmore

85. Reservoir Dogs

86. Grace Kelly

87. Alec Guinness

88. Idina Menzel

89. Beatrix Kiddo

90. Robert Zemeckis

150

91. 1994

92. Two

93. Cabaret

94. On Her Majesty's Secret Service

95. Hercules in New York

96. Red Dawn (1984)

97. Gone With the Wind

98. Avengers: Endgame

99. The Beverly Wilshire by Four Seasons

100. Midnight Cowboy

101. Harrison Ford

102. George Miller

103. Halle Berry

104. Red Apple cigarettes

105. Margaret Hamilton

06. Drew Barrymore

107. Rooster Cogburn

108. American Sniper

109. Three

110. Faye Dunaway and Warren Beatty

111. The Wolf of Wall Street

112. "Broadway Melody"

113. Bing Bong

114. Willem Dafoe

115. Syriana

116. Green

117. Linda Blair

118. It Happened One Night, One Flew Over the Cuckoo's Nest and The Silence of the Lambs.

119. USCSS Nostromo

120. 21

1. Whitney Huston
2. Diane
3. Hank Williams
4. Hunter
5. Charlie Chaplin
6. Anthony Hopkins
7. Hoskins
8. Spielberg
9. Stallone
10. Kiefer
11. Quentin
12. Kevin Costner
13. Nolte
14. Susan
15. Depp
16. He is an actor shooting an advert for whiskey
17. Francois Truffaut
18. Mandarin Chinese
19. Christmas Eve
20. Steve Buscemi
21. Deborah Moggach
22. Daft Punk
23. Welles plays himself
24. EVE
25. Jeff Bridges and Beau Bridges; Susie Diamond
26. Russell Crowe
27. Robert De Niro
28. Will Smith
29. Hilary Swank (in Boys Don't Cry)
30. Denzel Washington
31. Bobcat Goldthwait; Police Academy
32. Penelope Wilton and Bill Nighy; Spaced

33. A Jewish barber; Mussolini
34. A leopard
35. The Big Lebowski, vodka and Kalhua (or any coffee liqueur)
36. Or How I Learned to Stop Worrying and Love the Bomb
37. Steve Martin and Carl Reiner
38. Jaime Lee Curtis and Lindsay Lohan
39. As a star performer in NBA basketball
40. Duck Soup
41. Austin Powers: International Man of Mystery, Austin Powers: The Spy Who Shagged Me and Austin Powers in Goldmember, Mike Myers; Seth Green
42. Battleships; Cluedo, table, football, twister, Bergman's The Seventh Seal, in which the hero Knight plays Death at chess
43. Kate Beckinsale played Colin Farrel's false wife in 2012 version of Total Recall
44. John Carpenter and Kurt Russel
45. Hellboy, Hellboy 2; The Golden Army was the full title of the sequel
46. 80 days
47. Over the River Kwai
48. Ben Hur
49. Fantasia
50. Gone with the Wind
51. Bob Hope
52. Laurence Olivier

53. Brief Encounter
54. Hitchcock
55. Alec Guinness
56. Ealing Comedies
57. James Dean
58. Grace Kelly
59. Brigitte Bardot
60. Ten

61. Elizabeth Taylor
62. Dustin Hoffman
63. Rex Harrison
64. Oliver!
65. John Wayne
66. Mary Poppins
67. Peck
68. 101
69. Psycho
70. The Godfather
71. Superman
72. King Kong
73. Towering Inferno
74. Robert Redford
75. Moon

76. They directed the two versions of the Body Snatchers.

77. Sam Raimi, Ash

78. Christopher Lee and Peter Cushing

79. Dead of the Night

80. The Texas Chainsaw Massacre

81. The Innocents

82. Ringu (The Ring)

83. Peeping Tom
84. Bride of Frankenstein
85. 10.Peter Jackson
86. Let the Right One In
87. Regan
88. The Shining
89. His older sister Judith, seen killed in a flashback at the start of the movie

90. Near Dark

91. Lex Luthor

92. Simon Pegg; Eric Bana

93. Francois Truffaut

94. War of the Worlds (Spielberg) and King Kong (Jackson)

95. Robocop

96. Fritz Lang's Metropolis

97. Labyrinth

98. Rockatansky Toecutter

99. Richard Dreyfuss (the story goes that he virtually had to stalk Spielberg to get the part after the various big box office names turned it down)

100. James Cameron
101. Tron
102. Melanie Griffith
103. Twelve
104. Steven Soderbergh; George Clooney; Andrei Tarkovsky

105. Claude Rains; H.G. Wells

106. Tom Hanks.

107. Barnum.

108. Affleck and Damon.

153

109. Elizabeth Taylor.

110. Psycho.
111. Park.

112. Siam.

113. Dog.

114. Leonardo DiCaprio.

115. George.

116. Love.

117. Julia Roberts.

118. Attenborough.

119. West Side Story.

120. On the Roof.

121. Friel.

122. Bram Stoker's.

123. Dustin Hoffman.

124. Dolls.

125. Basinger.

126. Love Story.

127. Christie.

128. Gershwin.

129. The Bee Gees.

130. Alien.

131. Butch Cassidy &
      The Sundance Kid.

132. 70s.

133. Drew.

134. Costner.

135. The Silence of the Lambs.

136. WWII.

137. Woody Allen.

138. Austria.

139. Hepburn.

140. Grease.

141. Madonna.

142. Casablanca.

143. Titanic.

144. Clint Eastwood

145. Madagascar

146. Piano (The Piano and The Pianist)

147. Grease

148. Jurassic Park

149. Gone with the Wind

150. Meet the Parents

151. Marlon Brando and Robert DeNiro

152. Home Alone

153. Stephen Spielberg

154. Snow White and the Seven Dwarfs

155. Fantasia

156. Bambi

157. 101 Dalmatians

158. The Sword in the Stone

159. The Little Mermaid

160. Aladdin

161. Mulan

162. Tangled

163. Moana

164. Sylvester Stallone

165. Independence Day

166. Terminator

167. Die Hard

168. X-Men

169. The Predator

170. Bad Boys

171. Liam Neeson (Taken)

172. Mission Impossible

173. Deadpool

174. Maximus (Decimus Meridius in Gladiator)

175. Ocean's Eleven

176. Benjamin Button

177. Avatar

178. Quentin Tarantino

179. Hugh Grant

180. Lindsay Lohan

181 Javier Bardem

182. Mamma Mia!

183. Brokeback Mountain

184. Mary Poppins

185. Life is Beautiful

186. The Silence of the Lambs

187. Freddie Mercury

188. Natalie Portman

189. Meryl Streep

190. Tom Hanks (Forrest Gump and Philadelphia)

191. La La Land

192. Jack Nicholson

193. Best Actor and Best Actress winners from the same film

194. Alien

195. The Social Network

196. Jaws 2 (definitely not Jaws)

197. Dumb and Dumber

198. Shaun of the Dead

199. Psycho

200. E.T.

201. Ferris Bueller's Day Off
202. Ghostbusters
203. The Truman Show
204. Forrest Gump
205. The Post
206. Saving Mr Banks
207. Saving Private Ryan
208. Splash
209. Big
210. Joe vs the Volcano
211. A League of Their Own
212. The Da Vinci Code
213. Apollo 13
214. Pulp Fiction
215. Jaws
216. Apocalypse Now
217. Gone with the Wind
218. Titanic
219. The Godfather Part II
220. Dead Poets' Society
221. The Hunger Games
222. A Few Good Men
223. Castaway
224. Top Gun
225. The Sound of Music
226. Reservoir Dogs
227. The Bodyguard
228. Deliverance
229. Moulin Rouge
230. Dirty Dancing
231. Despicable Me 2
232. Trainspotting
233. The Wizard of Oz
234. Freddy Krueger
235. The Omen
236. The Blair Witch Project
237. Neve Campbell
238. Halloween
239. Friday 13th
240. Murder (redrum)
241. What you did last summer
242. The Birds
243. The Exorcist
244. 1994.
245. The Jazz
246. Morgan Freeman and Tim Robbins.
247. Red.
248. 9.
249. 6.
250. Tom Hanks.
251. Rudy.
252. Avatar.
253. Indiana Jones.
254. 1947.
255. Toy Story.
256. Snow White and the Seven Dwarfs.

257. Horror movie thriller movie.

258. 1994.

259. 1997.

260. Danny Ocean.

261. Star Wars: The Force Awakens.

262. The Hurt Locker.

263. The Lion King.

264. Mary Poppins.

265. Temple of Doom.

266. Roy Orbison.

267. Dr. No.

268. Sunbeam Alpine.

269. Agent J.

270. Dirty Dancing.

271. Pottery.

272. Rocky.

273. Almost $8 billion.

274. 59 films.

275. 2019.

276. Wes Craven.

277. Marion Crane.

278. 7.

279. 1.

280. Bubba Gump Shrimp Co.

281. Dead people.

282. Harlem Nights.

283. Sally Field.

284. Detective James Carter.

285. Bad Boys.

286. Indiana.

287. Chicago.

288. The Sausage King of Chicago.

289. 1964 Ferrari 250GT.

290. Matthew Broderick.

291. A record store.

292. The Breakfast Club.

293. Three fingers.

294. Quenten Tarrantino.

295. High School Musical.

296. Indiana Jones and the Kingdom of the Crystal Skull.

297. His high school basketball team.

298. Mulan.

299. 1967.

300. 8.

301. Red Dawn.

302. Joshua Ilan Gad.

303. Kevin Spacey.

304. Mrs. Doubtfire.

305. Chubbs.

306. 1994.

307. 7.

308. Fudge.

309. Mickey Mouse.

310. 4.

311. Jack Nicholson.

312. Katharine Hepburn.

313. Two righteous brothers.

314. The Terror of Tiny Town.

315. Grease.

316. Tom Hanks.

317. A piano.

318. Zoltan.

319. 8.5 hours.

320. Aspen.

321. A worm store.

322. Beauty and the Beast.

323. Frozen.

324. Mickey Mouse.

325. Lex Murphy.

326. A glass of water.

327. Illinois.

328. Uncle Buck.

329. Thanksgiving.

330. Harry and Marv.

331. Macaulay Culkin.

332. The House of the Devil in 1896.

333. Toy Story 3.

334. Indiana Jones.

335. Se7en.

336. Point Break.

337. Bodhi.

338. Sand.

339. Swingers.

340. Owen Wilson.

341. New Jersey.

342. From Dusk till Dawn.

343. Fight Club.

344. The 1960s.

345. Babe Ruth.

346. Titanic.

347. Space Jam.

348. Bedtime Stories.

349. 15.

350. Going back to school.

351. Almost Heroes.

352. 1992.

353. Garth.

354. The Exorcist and The Fly.

355. Aurora.

356. Dates.

357. Bicentennial Man.

358. What Dreams May Come.

359. 1991.

360. Home Alone.

01-B. Superman

02-A. Bruce Wayne

03-A. Gotham City

04-C. He was bitten by a spider
05-B. The Shadow
06-B. The Flash
07-C. Hulk
08-B. Wonder Woman
09-A. Kyle Rayner
10-C. Captain America
11-B. Catwoman
12-C. The Thing
13-A. Wonder Woman
14-A. Joker
15-C. The Atom
16-C. Spiderman
17-B. Daredevil

18-A. X-men

19-C. The police chief

20-A. A ring
21-C. Strom
22-A. The Paradise Island

23-B. Star City

24-B. Captain America

25-A. The Thing

26-A. Hawkeye
27-A. The Daily Bugle
28-C. Daredevil
29-C. Dr. Doom

30-Fly down his horns

31-A. Aquaman

32-B. Adamantium

33-A. Axis leaders

34-B. Galactus

35-A. Green Goblin

36-Psychology

37-C. Cosmic rays

38-B. Slowly fall

39-C. An archaeologist

40-B. Al Pacino

41-C. Kylo Ren

42-A. Itchy

43-B. Galactic Empire

44-B. Mechanic

45-B. Soap manufacturers
originally sponsored
these shows

46-C. The Archers

47-A. 1930

48-B. Liverpool

49-A. Neighbours
50-C. 3
51-B. Trumpet
52-B. Police officer

53-A. The Dog

54-C. Karen Taylor

55-C. Coronation Street

1. A horse
2. Orca
3. Anastasia & Drizella
4. Sidney Poitier
5. The Oscars
6. GoldenEye
7. 1962
8. Titanic
9. Steven Spielberg
10. Seven
11. Philadelphia (1994) & Forrest Gump (1995)
12. Snow White and the Seven Dwarfs
13. Mickey Mouse
14. Dinglehopper
15. Mulan
16. Han Solo
17. 6 million
18. Kyber Crystals
19. Randle Patrick McMurphy
20. Janet Gaynor
21. Betty White
22. Katherine Hepburn with 4 Academy Awards
23. Avenger: Endgame
24. Ellen DeGeneres
25. Frozen 2
26. Julie Andrews
27. Ivy
28. The Adventures of Priscilla Queen of the Desert
29. A whip
30. Temple of Doom
31. 12
32. 8.5 hours
33. 1984
34. Parasite
35. Whoopi Goldberg
36. Paul Newman
37. 1929
38. Six
39. Four times
40. Janet Gaynor & Fredric March
41. She has been nominated 21 times and won 3 Oscars
42. Pascal
43. Kevin Bacon
44. The Shining
45. 12
46. 1940
47. Cuff & Link
48. A rose
49. Bucklebury Ferry

50. New Zealand

51. 20

52. Death

53. "The Circle of Life"

54. Chimney Sweeper

55. Rhinoceros

56. 1997

57. Six

58. Kevin Spacey

59. Jane & Michael Banks

60. Convincing the world he didn't exist

61. A parrot

62. Matt Damon

63. WWII

64. 11

65. Whoopi Goldberg

66. Chippewa Falls, Wisconsin

67. "The Heart of the Ocean," a necklace

68. 41

69. Alfred Hitchcock

70. A nun

71. Phoenix, Arizona

72. He does not have a name

73. The Overlook Hotel

74. It is murder spelled backward

75. Rob Reiner

76. New York

77. 1986

78. Chicago

79. Two

80. Albert

81. He pulled a false fire alarm

82. Captain von Trapp

83. Gretl

84. Seven

85. A census taker

86. Dr. Chilton

87. 14

88. Katie

89. Hattie McDaniel

90. She fell off her pony

91. Bonnie

92. "Frankly, my dear, I don't give a damn."

93. Tara

94. 1994

95. 3 years, 2 months, 14 days, & 16 hours

96. 1982

97. Greenbow, Alabama

98. Benjamin Buford Blue

99. Gary Sinise

100. Forrest, Jr.

101. 25
102. DeLorean
103. 1994
104. Two
105. I hope
106. Ellis Boyd Redding
107. The Sisters
108. Ryan Reynolds
109. Joaquin Phoenix
110. Sitka
111. Legally Blonde
112. Mission Impossible: Rogue Nation
113. A Quiet Place
114. 25 lbs.
115. Underworld: Awakening
116. Will.i.am
117. Wyoming
118. Heath Ledger
119. A Ghostbusters lunchbox
120. Onions
121. Mater
122. A goose
123. Jordan Peele
124. Black Swan
125. Facebook
126. Robin Williams
127. Bruce, the shark
128. Five
129. Kinetic Energy
130. Three

131. The Reaping Day
132. Nightlock
133. Unbreakable, Split, & Glass
134. 2525
135. Rocky
136. Lex Murphy
137. The Hurt Locker
138. Arendelle
139. Eddie Redmayne
140. Renesmee
141. Cullen
142. Seven
143. Gryffindor, Slytherin, Ravenclaw, & Hufflepuff
144. Legolas
145. 1994
146. Mario Puzo
147. 40
148. Boyz n the Hood
149. Another Day of Sun
150. Avengers: Endgame

1. Lashana Lynch

2. Five – Saving Private Ryan, Catch Me If You Can, The Terminal, Bridge of Spies and The Post.

3. 12 Years a Slave

4. Sutton Hoo

5. The Princess Bride

6. 1995

7. James Cameron

8. Shaun of the Dead, Hot Fuzz, The World's End

9. Bong Joon-ho

10. Holly Hunter

11. Creed

12. The Iron Lady

13. Donny Osmond

14. Viggo Mortensen, whilst kicking a helmet.

15. Joe Versus the Volcano (1990), Sleepless in Seattle (1993) and You've Got Mail (1998)

16. Avengers: Endgame

17. Aragorn

18. Two (Titanic, Revolutionary Road)

19. A Few Good Men

20. Echo

21. Katherine Hepburn 4, Morning Glory (1933) Guess Who's Coming to Dinner (1967) The Lion in Winter (1968) On Golden Pond (1981)

22. Crimson Tide

23. Angelina Jolie

24. Michael Bay

25. That Thing You Do

26. The funeral of Gareth (played by Simon Callow)

27. Chadwick Boseman

28. Jordan Peele

29. The French Dispatch

30. From Russia With Love

31. Wingardium Leviosa

32. They are transformed into pigs

33. Paul Rudd

34. Despite being nominated 6 times, he has only won once in 2016 for The Revenant

35. Nicholas Hoult

36. The Blind Side

37. Jamaica

38. Gone with the Wind

39. Joni Mitchell

40. Michael Gambon

41. A box of chocolates

42. Pulp Fiction

43. Goldmember

44. Ron Burgundy

45. Obi-Wan Kenobi
the club at the start
of the film is called
Club Obi-Wan

46. Rick Blaine

47. Alan Smithee is an
official pseudonym
used by directors when
they want to disown a film
in other words, Alan
Smithee is credited
as director

48. He played a young
prostitute in Oscar
Wilde biopic Wilde

49. Sir Kenneth Branagh

50. Four (The Godfather:
Part 2, Heat, Righteous
Kill, The Irishman)

51. Seven Samurai

52. Hallie and Annie

53. Rear Window

54. Kathryn Bigelow

55. Ryan Gosling

56. Judge Doom
(Christopher Lloyd)

57. The Lion King

58. "Part of Your World"

59. Hans (Frozen)

60. Four feet long

61. Pocahontas

62. Ariel is the daughter
of Triton, who is the son
of Poseidon. Poseidon
is the brother of Zeus,
who is father to Hercules.

63. Pirates of the Caribbean:
At World's End

64. Elsa

65. Dumbo

66. Beauty and the Beast

67. Alicia Keys

68. Aladdin's

69. Daveigh Chase

70. 101 Dalmatians

71. Rapunzel

72. The Little Mermaid

73. Beauty and the Beast

74. Frozen

75. Toy Story

76. Aurora (Sleeping Beauty)

77. Pocahontas

78. Belle's

79. Bruce the vegetarian shark

01. 101 Dalmatians, Peter Pan, Lady, and the Tramp, Mulan, Hercules and Sleeping Beauty.

81. Mortimer

82. Ariel

83. Cinderella's dress transformation

84. Ariel

85. Aladdin

86. Hercules

87 Alyssa Milano

88. Christian Bale

89. Belle

90. Cinderella

91. Sleeping Beauty

92. Jackie Chan

93. Pumba

94. The Beatles

95. The evil queen

96. Aladdin

97. The Lion King

98. An apple

99. A clownfish and father of Nemo in the Disney movie Finding Nemo

100. Mary Gibbs

101. East of Eden, Rebel Without a Cause and Giant

102. Hans Zimmer

103. 2000

104. Santa's Super Sleigh

105. Frasier

106. Winter is Coming

107. The Woolpack

108. Jess and Max

109. Stranger Things

110. Baltimore

111. 52,101

112. Jesse Pinkman

113. Rosebud

114. Red
115. Schindler's List
116. Parasite

117. Matthew McConaughey and Woody Harrelson

118. Derek

119. The Banks family

120. Brad Pitt

Made in the USA
Columbia, SC
22 December 2024

50441220R00091